THE SECRETS OF
SUCCESSFUL ... &
L...

by

David M. Barber

♣
Cedar Publishing Limited
♣

© David Barber 2001
The right of David Barber to be identified as the author of this work has been asserted by him in accordance with the Copyright, Designs and Patents Act, 1988. All rights reserved, including the right of reproduction in whole or in part in any form except with the prior permission in writing of the publisher.

Cover illustration by Samatha Chaffey

Published by Cedar Publishing Limited
12 Pitch View
46 Kingsholm Road
Gloucester, GL1 3AU
01452 523727

ISBN 1-902654-03-X

Notice of Liability

While great care has been taken in the preparation of this publication, it should not be used as a substitute for appropriate professional advice. Neither the author nor Cedar Publishing can accept any liability for loss or damage occasioned by any person acting as a result of the material in this book.

Printed and bound in Great Britain by Bath Press Limited, Bath.

CONTENTS

What's This All About?

1. How Important Are Teaching And Leadership?   5
2. What Is The Purpose Of Teaching And Leadership?   7
3. Surely, I Need Talent To Be A Good Teacher And Leader?   13
4. <u>Every</u> Distributor Is A Leader!   16
5. How Can I Be A Teacher And Leader From Day One?   18
6. Treat Your Business With The Seriousness It Deserves   22
7. As A Leader, Focus On Your Group Not On Yourself   24
8. How Much Distributors Do Is More Important Than How Well They Do It   26
9. Do Not Put Your Aspirations Onto Other People!   29
10. Keep People Working Within Their Comfort Zones   31
11. Make Sure Your People Are Always Accompanied In Everything They Do!   34
12. How To Be A Great Teacher   41
13. How To KISS. The Essence Of Great Teaching   46
14. How To Be A Great Leader   50

'What Do I Do Next?'   58

What's This All About?

The Secrets Of Successful Teachers & Leaders is the fourth book in *The Secrets Series*, a home learning programme which is an essential tool for new distributors. The full series is:

- *Just What Is...... Network Marketing?* (a recruiting tool)
- *The Distributor's Action Plan*
- *The Secrets Of Successful Sponsors*
- *The Secrets Of Successful Teachers & Leaders* (this book)
- *The Secrets Of Successful Group Structuring*.

It is very important to read these in the correct order. As this book is the fourth in *The Secrets Series*, you should not go any further unless you have already read the first three, *Just What Is...... Network Marketing?*, *The Distributor's Action Plan* and *The Secrets Of Successful Sponsors*. As you recruit people, make sure that they, too, follow the series through.

Teaching and Leadership are two of the **Income-Producing Activities (or IPAs)** around which successful network marketing revolves. The IPAs were laid out in the Introduction to *The Secrets Of Successful Sponsors*. Because the IPAs are those activities which contribute to a distributor's success, your teaching and leadership should revolve around them. So it is worth reminding you that each of them is in their way essential (the IPAs are in bold): if your group does not **sponsor,** it will not grow. If it does not **retail,** no-one earns anything. If you don't **teach** or **lead** your group properly, or **structure** it right, the growth will be too slow, the sales will be too low and the drop out rate will be too high.

> **So sponsoring starts the process**
> ⇒ **retailing produces the income**
> ⇒ **teaching, leading and structuring
>   your group maximise that income**

If your network lays on Business Opportunity Meetings (BOMs), trainings or events then you should add a sixth IPA: **Selling Events,** which will also help to maximise your income.

What is the difference between teaching and leadership?

The difference can be confusing, so let's see the defining lines. Leadership actually covers three responsibilities:

Leadership = motivation + direction + **teaching**

So teaching is simply part of leadership, albeit a fundamental part. (Direction in simple terms means ensuring that your group is going in the same direction as your company, and that everyone is 'singing from the same hymn sheet').

Leadership refers to your relationship with the whole of your group. But, as well as running your group, you should also be working in a 'hands on' way with just a few, maybe not more than five or six of your people. Some of these may be new distributors and you are helping them to get their groups established. Others may be experienced, established distributors who need very close help from you in a variety of ways; in these latter cases, you may be more of a **mentor** than a leader.

Teaching is specifically concerned with job training, a very important part of which, where network marketing is concerned, is to teach your distributors in turn how to lead and teach their groups.

There are two aspects to teaching. One is on-the-job training, which some people refer to as **coaching** but which we talk about as **accompanying people in everything they do.** The other is off-the-job or arm's-length training: discussions on the phone, training through manuals and bulletins, 'classroom' trainings (which may take place on a one-to-one basis or in small groups in hotel foyers or people's homes), seminars and sizzle sessions.

Therefore **teaching** is what you do with your whole group. **Coaching,** for those who use that term, is part of teaching and only applies with the handful of distributors with whom you will be working on an individual basis—or accompanying in everything they do.

Teaching and leadership also require different skills to each other. Some people are more naturally good leaders, others are more naturally good teachers. If you want to do the best you can for your distributors, you can, and should, learn to be good at both. And you can.

The importance of personal development

Although the IPAs are the activities which you and your distributors need to carry out, how well people carry them out will depend on their attitudes to the IPAs, to themselves, to their success and to life. In fact, although *The Secrets Series* is about technique,

> **Attitude is far more important than technique both to your success and to the success of your people**

People simply cannot succeed without the right attitudes. This gets us into the fascinating realm of **Personal Development,** which helps us to develop those attitudes.

Although you, as a teacher and leader, may not need personal development to get your attitudes right, I can assure you that most of your people will! So even if you do not need to become an expert for yourself, you will for them. Either of my books *Network Marketeers... Supercharge Yourself!* or *How To Achieve Everything You've Ever Wanted* will help you get started and show you what to teach.

If you have never taught anyone before, or if you have never been in a position of leadership, don't worry! *Everyone* can become a good teacher and leader if they want to. There is nothing difficult to learn and, by the end of this book, you will know just how to be a great leader and teacher.

The rewards of teaching and leadership are huge. Leaving aside the effect on your income, the satisfaction of seeing your people improve under your teaching and blossom under your leadership...... well, there is no feeling like it! Some would say that when, through your efforts, you turn someone from failure to success, or you see people who have had a really bad time come into your group and have their lives turned around to become happy, fulfilled and successful, it is even more satisfying than sex!

Perhaps I would not go that far. But I hope that, through this book, I will help you to experience for yourself the joys of teaching and leadership.

Chapter One

How Important Are Teaching And Leadership?

Network marketing is defined as many things:
a sponsoring business...... a showing business...... a teaching business...... a retail business...... a lifestyle opportunity ...... a self-development business...... a business for anyone and everyone...... perhaps you have come across other definitions.

All of these definitions are right in their context. But I think that it is primarily a teaching and leadership business because

Above all, your level of success will be determined by how well you teach and lead your group

Obviously, many other factors will come into your success and we cover these throughout *The Secrets Series*. But if you do not teach and lead your group in a positive way, and if you do not also respond in a positive way to the teaching and leadership your uplines give you, much of your effort will be wasted.

As an upline, you wield immense power

You now have the power to turn people from failure into success. Equally, if you do not use your position wisely, you have the power to turn people, who would have succeeded under better leadership, into failures

So get away from the thinking of so many managers in business—those whose only concern is for themselves and their superiors—or so many corporate leaders, whose only concern is for their shareholders and, again, for themselves.

Get away, too, from the thinking of modern society which makes it acceptable to have authority without responsibility, or the perks of a position without the commitment and duties which should go with it.

Leadership means responsibility. It means accepting the responsibility of doing everything you can to help the distributors in your group to succeed

However, although you should go all the way for people who are both willing to learn and to apply your advice, don't feel responsible for people who will not help themselves. Do your best to get them to help themselves but, in the final analysis:

Your responsibility is to show people what to do, but it is their responsibility to decide what to do with that

Therefore, with your responsibility goes the proviso that you are only responsible for those who do their best to help themselves.

With authority goes accountability. If someone's application is wrong because your advice is wrong, the responsibility is yours. And if they fail as a result, that, too, is your responsibility.

However, the plus side is that, if they succeed, that is also because of you!

Chapter Two

What Is The Purpose Of Teaching And Leadership?

What are we trying to achieve as teachers and leaders? Several things:

1. To get to the income we want as fast as we can

Whether the income you want from network marketing is low or high, presumably you would like to reach it as soon as possible, given the hours that you devote to your network marketing business. You will get there more quickly by turning yourself into a good group leader and teacher.

2. To help our distributors achieve the incomes they want as fast as they can

In *The Secrets Of Successful Sponsors* we established that we can only achieve the income we want through our distributors (the Keystone Law). In other words:

> **We can only achieve what we want by helping the distributors in our group to achieve what they want**

They, too, would probably like to achieve the incomes they want as fast as they can. Again, if you are a good teacher and leader you will get them there more quickly.

3. To turn failures into successes

Our job is to teach people how to be successful. But what is the definition of success? It is the satisfaction of strongly felt desires, whatever these may be. If a distributor needs £50 a month through their business to create or maintain the lifestyle they want, and they achieve it, they are a success. If a distributor needs £50,000 a month to create or maintain the lifestyle they want, and they manage only £45,000, they are not yet a success.

If we are talking about distributors to whom success is reaching a very high income, only a very small number, possibly only one in 2,000, can reach the top without learning the business properly. They follow Mark Twain's philosophy: 'All you need is ignorance and confidence, and then success is sure.' But Mark Twain neglected to mention that this only applies to natural motivators able to build groups on the power of their personality alone. Or people with exceptional determination and patience who know that, if they hang on for long enough, they are bound to make it. Or, let's face it, luck! Some top distributors happened to be in the right place and the right time, and happened to be lucky with the people who came into their group. The one thing common to all these types is that they have not achieved their success by finding routes to the top which work for everyone—only for those who can match their natural leadership abilities, or determination and patience, or luck.

Where does that leave the other 1,999 distributors which by the law of averages almost certainly includes *YOU?!* Not very far. Unless, of course, you do take the time and trouble to find a way to the top which will work for everyone who wants to follow it, and make this the culture of your group.

If you do this, you will be able to 'turn water into wine'. You will be able to turn people, who would have failed without your expertise, into successes.

4. To make this truly a business for everyone

Although network marketing is supposed to be a business for everyone, it very rarely is because few uplines are good enough to make it so.

Where teaching is concerned, many people who think they are good, are not. The sum total of their expertise is, 'Copy what I have done, and you, too, will succeed.' There is only one problem with this: these distributors usually have natural leadership qualities or exceptional patience and determination, or they are just plain lucky. If you do not have one or other of these attributes, can you copy them?

As we said above, only about one in 2,000 distributors have these qualities. A good teacher is someone who knows how to show the other 1,999 the way to success.

The same applies to leadership. A general who wins battles is of course a successful general. But is he a good leader if he is wasteful of the lives of his men? Or, to be a good leader, must he also win battles with the minimum loss of life?

In the same way, because someone has built a large group, it does not mean that they are a good leader. Perhaps most big group leaders built their group on the bones of an unnecessarily high failure rate. When I say unnecessarily high, I mean that there were failures who could have succeeded had they had the right training and leadership. Is that a good leader? Or is a good leader one who has built their group with the minimum failure rate possible and the maximum number of successes possible?

Although we know that the biggest reason for failure is that people do not do what is necessary, that doesn't get us away from the fact that there is a difference between someone failing *because of* us—because we did not give them the right guidance—and someone who fails *despite* us, in other words, we had the right strategy in place for them but they refused our help.

Too often, uplines claim as a success someone who would have got there anyway. But that is not a success. The only real success is someone who, without your help, would have failed. That is the only true test of a teacher and leader.

5. To keep people focused on the IPAs

When you analyse how distributors spend the time they devote to the business, you will be amazed at how much of it is spent on non-IPAs. Check yourself, too, because if you spend valuable time on activities which are not focused on your success, you can hardly blame your people for doing so!

The only *productive* work in network marketing is making Get-Active phone calls, taking people through the sponsoring process, helping them establish successful businesses, and retailing

---

The more time your group spends on those activities, the sooner you will all reach the incomes you want. That is why I said in the Introduction that your teaching and leadership should revolve round the IPAs and personal development. This means as far as possible discouraging non-IPAs.

The reason why people get side-tracked into other activities is either because of inertia or because they find some of the IPAs —particularly the Get-Active phone calls—tough to carry out. So they compensate by finding other jobs to do. These jobs may make them feel as if they are doing something positive, but they are not.

This is not something which is peculiar to network marketing: almost all enterprises are filled with people taking the easy way out instead of doing what the job requires them to do.

I'm no different! Although I love the feeling of contribution my books make to people's lives and success, I absolutely hate writing them! So I find any excuse not to. I make 'important' phone calls, and then stay on the phone longer than I should. Problems around the house which I have happily lived with for months now suddenly need my 'urgent' attention. I make cups of tea I don't really want. I convince myself that I need a breath of fresh air 'to clear my head'. In fact, I come up with any plausible reason I can not to have to sit at my word processor.

So it is not always a case of someone not being prepared to work; some people work very hard and put in long hours at jobs which are not worthwhile. The problem is that they are working hard, but they are not working smart.

The silly thing is that all this prevarication we are so good at doesn't stop a particular task from having to be done! It simply postpones it. At some stage, my book has still got to be written; a distributor's contact list and their ATAC Lifeplan and FOOD Card have still got to be drawn up. Those Get-Active phone calls still have to be made. Whatever job we are prevaricating over, we still have to do it, or fall by the wayside. All we achieve is that our success (if we haven't manage to kill it by our prevarication) comes later than it need have, and we look back with regret on the time wasted.

Therefore, one of the most important jobs you can do as an upline is to help your people stay focused on the IPAs. This is a difficult task. Nevertheless, the more they do now, the sooner they will get to the income they want, and the sooner you will get to the income you want. Do you know the only real difference between successful people and the rest of us?

They get on with it! While we are thinking about doing what needs to be done, successful people are doing it

---

One solution is to get people to write out exactly how they used the time they spent on the business last week. Until people do this, they will not accept that there is a problem. Most will be horrified to discover how little really productive work they did!

Once they accept the problem, give them the cure: at the end of each week, get them to write out their **Weekly Plan** for the following week. This consists of the days and hours they will set aside for their network marketing business, and exactly how they are going to fill that time. Then, in discussion with you, they have to justify that use of time.

But this must start with you!

Do your weekly plan, so that you can show your people what a difference it makes to your *productive* work.

Chapter Three

Surely, I Need Talent To Be A Good Teacher And Leader?

There is a belief that not everyone can teach or lead; that good teachers and, particularly, leaders are born, not made. This is not so. We all, everyone of us, can both teach and lead. There is no mystery attached to it.

Let's look at the two things separately. First, teaching. Could you show someone the way to your local shops? Yes? Then you are *teaching* them the way to the shops. Could you explain the meaning of a word you know to someone else? Then you are *teaching* them the meaning of that word. Could you explain the plot of a film you have just seen to someone who has not seen it? Then you are *teaching* them the plot. What about your favourite pastime; could you show or explain it to other people? Then you are *teaching* them.

We said in *The Secrets Of Successful Sponsors*:

This is a showing business

We were referring then to sponsoring. But we can equally apply that comment to teaching:

Teaching is showing or explaining

We can all show or explain things to people. This book will simply show you how to do it better.

With regard to leadership, that, too, is something of which everyone is capable. To show how true that is, let me pose you a question: if a child of yours went missing and you were unable to contact any of the emergency services, do you have any doubt that you could round up the neighbours and passers-by into a very effective search and rescue mission? That is leadership, and I have never met anyone who doubted their ability to lead under those circumstances. If you can be a leader under those circumstances, you have the ability to be the leader of a network marketing group.

So what does successful leadership need? As the example of a missing child shows,

---
Successful leadership needs a common purpose important enough for those present to want to get involved
---

The rescue of a child is that important. But the rescue of your pet slug is probably not; if anyone wanted to organise a rescue for that, they would need considerable leadership skill!

An important common purpose is there, too, in network marketing, because most distributors sign up to achieve something which matters to them. In *The Secrets Of Successful Sponsors*, we called this a strongly felt desire. If someone feels part of an important common purpose or has a strongly felt desire, they will listen to the most uncharismatic people and follow the most unlikely leaders if they think that those people can help them achieve what they want.

Having said that, if you want to be successful at teaching or leading a distributor, you will need to create a positive, close relationship with them. Before you can *teach*, you need a person's ear, in other words their willingness to listen to you. If people are prepared to listen to you, they are prepared to learn from you. Before you can *lead*, you need a person's loyalty. If they feel loyal to you, they will follow you. A successful relationship means that a distributor *wants* you to teach them, or *is happy* for you to lead them.

So a leader has to have the ability to create loyalty? Surely, that must require charisma or some leadership talent? Actually, no. You do need some attributes, but these are nothing to do with talent, or even skill.

What makes people happy for you to teach and lead them? The secret is simple. It lies in how much they like, trust and respect you, and how much they feel that you have their interests at heart and respect them

---

If you refer back to *The Secrets Of Successful Sponsors*, you will see that these are the very same attributes you need to be a top-flight recruiter. And the truly wonderful thing about the attributes we need to be good teachers and leaders is that they are all free, given to us by a bounteous God or nature!

How do you get people to like, trust and respect you as a teacher and leader? And how do you show them that you have their interests at heart and respect them? Take five easy steps:

1. Learn your subject, which breaks down into:
   - Your opportunity, product and marketplace
   - The concept of network marketing
   - Personal development. As we discussed in the Introduction, people cannot succeed without the right attitudes.
2. Learn how to teach and lead distributors
3. Accept responsibility as an upline to help them succeed
4. Really care about their success
5. Show them your respect, both as human beings and for the purposes they hope to achieve through network marketing.

Is there anything here you would find difficult? Yet these five steps are all it takes to become as good a teacher and leader as you will ever need to be to reach the top. The only question is whether you have the motivation to take them.

Chapter Four

Every Distributor Is A Leader!

We have been speaking about your need to be a teacher and leader. But, in addition to being a part of your group, each of your distributors also heads up their own group. Therefore, the same must apply to them:

The success of every one of your distributors depends on how well they teach and lead their group

So it is an important part of your job to stress to your people how important it is for them, too, to learn to teach and lead their individual groups.

In fact, you owe it to them because until a distributor accepts their responsibilities of leadership they are unlikely to build a successful group, and they won't reach their full potential.

The more you get every distributor to accept their responsibility as a leader, the faster your business will grow

There is no denying that the biggest reason for failure is that distributors, for whatever reason, are not prepared to do what is necessary. What is not sufficiently understood is that,

A significant number of distributors fail because they are very willing to do what is necessary, but they do not know what to do and their uplines do not know how, or what, to teach them

Too many uplines do not accept responsibility for the people in their group. Do you want to be like them, or would you rather learn how to do the business properly and ensure that every distributor in your group is given that same opportunity? Having said that, many will not take our advice.

> *Do you know the best slimming diet in the world? You can eat what you like when you like, and as much as you like. It is an amazingly easy diet to stick to, but it doesn't work.*

Many distributors approach this business in the same way: they do what they like when they like and how they like. It is an easy strategy to stick to, but it doesn't work! So why do they persist in doing it? For three reasons:

- They are unteachable. Some will remain unteachable no matter what we do
- They do not take the business seriously enough. We will come back to this in Chapter Six
- *No-one explained to them that they have responsibilities as leaders.* So let's explain it to them:

The minute a distributor sponsors someone, they hold that person's future in their hands.

Not all leaders are equal

Although we say that every distributor has to become a leader, there are different degrees of leadership. The onus of leadership on a distributor who needs only a handful of people in their group to earn what they want is obviously very much less than the onus on a distributor who is aiming for an income of tens of thousands of pounds a month.

However, there are certain minimum requirements which every distributor, whether they want to be major or minor leaders, needs to fulfil, and we will cover these in the next chapter.

Chapter Five

How Can I Be A Teacher And Leader From Day One?

While you are new to the business you will hardly know the concept better than the people who are coming into your group. And you will not yet have had much practical experience of what works and what does not. Yet, by asking people to join your group, you are already responsible as their teacher and leader whether you accept it or not. Some of these people may be good friends, relatives or neighbours of yours, and you won't want to let them down.

Unfortunately, if you are an experienced businessperson or salesperson, your previous experience is unlikely to be of much benefit to you yet. Whatever we have done before, we are all equally inexperienced when we start in network marketing. So what can we do? How can we overcome our inexperience in network marketing?

Take these four positive steps:

1. Support your uplines
2. Learn as a teacher
3. Really, deeply care, in your heart, about the success of your people
4. Be a good example to your people of how a good distributor should learn and do the job.

Let's look at each of these in turn.

1. Support your uplines

The best solution is to find an upline to help you. But, even if you do, there is not a lot they can do unless you let them! Many distributors hold their group close to their chest as if it is their property. Others question everything an upline suggests, or they pick the bits of advice they like the sound of and reject the rest. If you are like this, don't be surprised if your upline decides to leave you to your own devices.

Apart from any upline you can find to help you, you may find that the company or your uplines run trainings, meetings, BOMs (Business Opportunity Meetings), and events of all sorts. You will remember that, if they do, it is a sixth IPA that you **Sell Events** (see page 2). Get your distributors to support them. Encourage them to learn the business properly by plugging them into all the company or upline activities available to help them succeed.

'What if I cannot find an upline to help me?'

If you cannot find an upline to help, or your upline group does not run trainings or BOMs, don't worry. Many people have become successful despite being unable to find adequate upline support; it's just harder, that's all. Network marketing is a very forgiving business for those who take it seriously and take the time and the trouble to learn the business properly.

Your solution is to do exactly what you are doing now: encourage your new people to use *The Secrets Series*, and set out to learn *together* to apply the principles we discuss. Do this, and you can still build a business with a solid base.

2. Learn as a teacher

Many distributors see themselves as the only teacher of their group. Not so: because every distributor heads up their own group, *every* distributor is also the teacher of their own group. So, whenever you learn something, make sure that you pass that priceless information on to your people with instructions that they, too, as teachers in their own right, pass it on to theirs.

A good tip, whenever you are out with a downline, or one of your people phones you for advice, or you run a meeting, is to say: 'Before we start, just remember that everything we discuss you will at some stage have to teach your people.' This constantly stresses to your team that we are, all of us, learning all the time as *teachers*.

3. Really, deeply care, in your heart, about the success of your people

Leadership is not just about what people think of you, it is about what you think of them and,

---
Action = Reaction. People will react to you in response to the way you act towards them

---

Whatever you think of a distributor, they are in your group. If you want to get the best out of them, be proud of them, give them the respect due to all human beings, encourage them and support them.

Caring enough about people *to want to make them succeed* is the single most important attribute to great leadership

---

As the great Zig Ziglar says: 'People do not care what you know, until they know that you care...... about *them!*'

Caring about people's success means that, for their benefit, you learn the job properly.

> *While a man was working on the railway, a train came speeding round the corner. He ran as fast as he could down the track, but the train finally caught up with him and hit him.*

When he regained consciousness, the nurse asked him why he hadn't simply run up the embankment. 'Don't be silly!' he said. 'If I couldn't outrun it on the flat, what chance would I have running uphill?'

This man suffered from lack of knowledge. If we as teachers and leaders don't learn, we, too, will lead our people down the track, waiting to be hit by the train of failure.

4. Be a good example to your people of how a good distributor should learn and do the job

This means *Lead by example*. Network marketing is not like normal business in which the attitude of many managers is, 'Do what I say, not what I do!' No matter how good we are at teaching our people the right things to do, it will not work for us unless we *Practise what we preach*.

There is a reason for this: the way in which our distributors learn is governed by what is called **The Theory of Duplication,** one rule of which states: *Our people will copy what we DO, not what we SAY*. If we don't do, our people won't either, no matter what we say.

If you are working with an experienced upline, leading by example means just doing what he or she asks you to do, and then passing that example to your people. Don't worry if, at this stage, you cannot do it well. The really important thing is to do it, and to do it to the best of your ability. In this business, doing things badly is very much better than not doing them at all. So if you haven't yet got started, you've no excuse. Get started now!

Chapter Six

Treat Your Business With The Seriousness It Deserves

As a teacher and leader, your group will take their lead from you as to how seriously to take the business. If you do not give it due importance, nor will they.

Almost all of us undervalue this great business because entry is so easy: in what other occupation can people join without any form of job interview or selection, with no references, with no previous experience, and with no competition for places?

Ease of entry also means low cost of entry. In what other *high* level business can we start with minimal cost and none of the cashflow problems associated with funding growth? Of course, if our opportunity has a tangible product (i.e., something people can see and buy) we need a good range of samples to show, we might need some sales aids, and we should invest in books, tapes, videos and seminars on network marketing, to teach both ourselves and our group. But there is a huge difference between the investment required for that and the finance needed to buy and hold loads of stock for sale.

But ease of entry has a downside: *Easy come, easy go* is a killing attitude. Because it is so easy to get started, probably the majority of distributors do not take their businesses seriously enough. With so much to go for, that is a real shame.

I often ask *serious* distributors if they think they are working really hard at their network marketing business. Of course they say yes, and they mean it. Then I ask: are they putting in as much effort as they would have done had they borrowed

£100,000 and put their house on the line? To their surprise, most realise that they are not. Ask yourself: are you? Another question:

> **Are they imposing on themselves the same disciplines of work as an employer would impose on them? Are *you*?**

You see, even those of us who think we are working hard can get seduced into taking the business less seriously because of the ease of entry. If we can be affected like that, what chance has everyone else?

This business is not an easy option, and if anyone wants to succeed they must be more disciplined and more determined than if they were employed, not less so. So teach your group to treat our business with the seriousness it deserves. How? Teach them to judge it by its *real* value to them.

What is the real value of our opportunity?

To make it possible for us to live life the way we want. If we need £4,000 a year out of network marketing to fund our lifestyle then this is a £4,000 a year business. If we need £40,000 a year, this is a £40,000 a year business. If we need £400,000 a year, this is a £400,000 a year business—not the few pounds it cost to join. So its real value is not the *input*, it is the *output*:

> **Value the business by what it can do for you, not by what it costs to join**

That is why network marketing is often called a lifestyle, not a business, opportunity. If we want a more committed group, we must make sure that our people value the business properly.

Chapter Seven

As A Leader, Focus On Your Group Not On Yourself

As we learnt in *The Secrets Of Successful Sponsors,*

Your ONLY path to success lies through your people

Because it is so fundamental to success, we called this **The Keystone Law.**

From the Keystone Law, you can see that your success will lie not in how good you are at sponsoring or at retailing, but in how much sponsoring and retailing are going on in your group. You can be as good as you like at both these IPAs, but you will never earn much more than an average income, if that. This may be enough if you are in network marketing to earn a part-time income or if you are happy with low earnings, but even at that level you will be working harder than you need if you rely purely on your own sponsoring or retailing activities.

If you want to earn the income you need more easily, or if you want to get into the higher earning brackets, it will be the sponsoring and retailing efforts of your group as a whole, not what you do, which will get you there. That means:

Your level of success will depend entirely on other people

And how well they do will depend entirely on how well they are taught and led. This in turn will depend on the culture of teaching and leadership you create in your group. This should (a) cut out the need for talent as much as possible, and (b) make the business as easy as possible. That way, you reduce the drop-outs to a minimum and you maximise the successes.

You will only succeed in this if you focus on your group's abilities, not your own. No matter how well you can carry out any or all of the IPAs, the important thing is *can the least experienced, least talented, least confident slowest learners in your group* succeed in them? If they can, you have cracked it, and you will, I promise you, reach the high-earning levels!

The more you apply the new perspective of making your group not yourself the issue, the better. For instance, what is the real value of *The Secrets Series*? Does it lie in what *you* learn from it? No, the real value of the series is as a teaching aid for your group, not as a learning aid for you.

Chapter Eight

How Much Distributors Do Is More Important Than How Well They Do It

Your gardener is immensely strong, and can wield a mighty spade. Your granny can dig only with a trowel. On the face of it, who would you put your money on to finish digging the garden first?

Then you learn that your gardener digs only a few spadefuls a day before giving up, as many people do in life, whereas granny with her little trowel just keeps going on hour after hour, at her own gentle pace. Who will you put your money on now?

You may not know much about sport, but I bet you know the answer to this question: you are the manager of a football club, and you have the choice of playing either a brilliant player who has to be constantly goaded into action, or someone who is not so good, but who never stops trying and chasing all over the pitch. Which will you pick?

In network marketing, *doing* the job is always more important than how *well* we do it

Network marketing does not reward people who put in occasional flashes of brilliance and then die away. Our history is full of greatly talented people who came in, made huge ripples in the pond but, also like ripples, disappeared without trace. We are not in a sprint, we are in a marathon, a marathon in which *everyone* who crosses the finishing line to create the life they want for themselves is a winner. The winners are the distributors who put in consistent effort week after week, just like granny with her trowel, doing the things that need to be done.

Whenever we are in a teaching situation, we should keep our group focused on this very important reality:

> **Only when someone is doing, is there any point in finding ways to do better**

What does this mean in practice? That we do as much of the basic activities of network marketing as we can, in the time we devote to the business:

- The more Get-Active phone calls we make, the more people we will show our opportunity to ⇒
- The more people we show the opportunity to, the more people will join our business ⇒
- The more people we show the product to, the more people will buy ⇒
- The more distributors we work with on the above three activities, the greater the production of our group will be, the higher the number of successful distributors we will create, and the lower our drop-out rate will be.

What turns action to *successful* action is attitude

The only rider we would add is that, whatever action a distributor takes, they must take it with the right attitude. Two people can take exactly the same action. One will succeed while the other will fail. What makes the difference? Attitude. For example, we can make a sponsoring phone call in two ways. The first is this:

'Hello Mary. David here. I've just come across this amazing business opportunity, and I really think you should have a look at it. When can I come over and see you?'

The second is this:

'Hello Mary! David here! I've just come across this amazing business opportunity, and I really think you should have a look at it! When can I come over and see you?'

The words may be exactly the same, but which distributor do you think will be the more successful?

Indeed, action taken with the wrong attitude is often actually worse than taking no action at all, because you are wasting valuable time. In our example, is a distributor who makes sponsoring phone calls with the lack of enthusiasm and belief shown in the first phone call ever going to sign anyone up?

Apply something half-heartedly, and we will get what we deserve: a half result, or failure

Having said that, if a distributor is prepared to make phone calls and is prepared to be taught, you can teach them to make effective phone calls no matter how bad they are now. And they will sign people up. But the best phone caller in the world will not sign anyone up unless they are prepared to make calls in the first place. As we said earlier:

Only when someone is doing, is there any point in finding ways to do better.

Chapter Nine

Do Not Put Your Aspirations Onto Other People!

You will notice that we refer frequently to helping people to achieve what *they* want. This is one big difference between network marketing and most other forms of business. In traditional business, our job is to achieve what our employer wants us to achieve. They decide our hours of work, what our targets will be, and how much we earn.

In network marketing, distributors make these decisions for themselves. They decide the working hours, they decide what their targets will be, and they decide how much they want to earn.

It is our job to help people achieve what they want, even if it happens to be far less than we want them to achieve
---

A woman and her husband had to interrupt their holiday to go to the dentist. She said the dentist: 'I want a tooth pulled, but I'm in a hurry, so I don't want an anaesthetic. Just pull the tooth as fast as you can, and we'll be on our way.'

'Good heavens!' the dentist said. 'You are a brave woman! Tell me which tooth it is, and I'll do the job as fast as I can.'

The woman turned to her husband and said, 'Show him which tooth it is, dear!'

In our anxiety to achieve our own goals, we can intentionally or unintentionally put pressure on people to do what we want, not what they want. This is a normal way for managers to behave in traditional business. Indeed, they are expected to behave in this way. In traditional business, we are told what to do and how to do it. And it is easy for managers to make us do what they want because, if we don't, we get fired.

In fact, in network marketing, this is just the wrong way to go about things. If we pile our aspirations onto distributors, rather than help them shoulder their own, or if we make them feel inadequate because they are not keeping up with our expectations, we make them more likely to drop out. Pressure may make people do less, not more.

Every network marketing distributor is boss of their own group. As such, they have the right to run their business in any way they see fit, and this may not be the way we want them to. This puts an extra pressure on us as uplines, because we cannot make anyone do anything. Instead, we have to encourage them to want to learn and to run their businesses in the best way.

Chapter Ten

Keep People Working Within Their Comfort Zones

It is obvious that the way to earn as much as we want as fast as we can is not only to help the group recruit more people, but also to help the distributors who are already on board to do as well as possible. Many people think that the way to do this is to exhort their distributors to work outside their comfort zones.

Although this sounds good, it is not the best way to help inactive people become active, or active people to become more active. Indeed, it may have the opposite effect, because very few people will work outside their comfort zone for anything other than a temporary period.

Let's look at the reality of our group. In simple terms, we will have two sorts of distributor: 10% who are self-motivated, and 90% who are not. And each needs to be treated in a different way:

- 10% will be self-motivated and want to work outside their comfort zone. So we help them to do so because that is where they are happiest
- The other 90% are the opposite: they work better inside their comfort zone. If we try to push them outside it, we will actually encourage them to drop out.

The way to get results out of those 90% is for us to apply the rule that *Network marketing is a lot of people doing a little bit*. So we accept them as they are and we find ways of getting something out of them, no matter how little it may be.

It is easy to do this: we ask distributors to set their own targets. Even if these are much lower than we would like, we must show that we are happy with them. We must make sure that distributors do not feel consciously or subconsciously pressured to set their targets higher than they want, otherwise they will soon stop going for them.

Once a target is set, we should not assume that a distributor will stick to it because, if the target turns out to be too high, they will soon give up; or, more often, simple inertia sets in. So we keep in regular touch—daily to start with. Now, if they fall down on their target, we are on hand to suggest they reduce it. And we continue to do that until a point is reached when they can keep to their target. If we make sure that the suggestion to reduce the target comes from us, we remove the feeling of failure people have when they find they cannot keep up with what they have set themselves.

Let's take an example. A distributor sets themselves a target of five sponsoring calls a day. If in hindsight this proves difficult, they do not normally just reduce the calls to a number they feel comfortable with, they are more likely to stop entirely. But if we help them to reduce their target to a point where they can keep it up day after day, they might still keep making calls.

We might end up with one call a day by a distributor, which does not sound much. But that is still 30 a month. Three calls a week is still 12 a month. That is probably considerably more than the 90% in our group are currently making! And look at the contribution to our group's activity: if we have 100 distributors each making three calls a week, that is 1,200 calls a month promoting our business. And all because we helped them to work within their comfort zones.

The importance of appreciation

Very importantly, make people feel that their contribution is valued, *no matter how little it is*:

'Hello, Fred. Have you done your three calls this week?' 'Yes.' 'Well done! That's excellent!'

If a person sets a high target and fails to reach it, they feel they are a failure. If they set a low target and achieve it, they feel they are a success
---

We can apply the same strategy to retailing. If we help people to retail what they feel they can comfortably do, no matter how little it is, our group retailing will go up, not down.

If your product is suitable for parties, you can use the same strategy there: get people to set targets they know they can handle. If you have 100 distributors in your group who never organise parties and they agree to one party each every four months, that will give you an extra 25 parties per month. With parties averaging £200, that means an extra £5,000 group volume per month.

The other way to increase people's activity is to encourage them to work with other people, never on their own. This is the subject of our next chapter.

Chapter Eleven

Make Sure Your People Are Always Accompanied In Everything They Do!

Of all the techniques of teaching and leadership, this is by far the most important. If we understand that this is a warm market business,

> Getting the income we want as fast as we can is really about getting everyone in our group to reach as many names on their contact list as fast as possible

That means increasing work rates. This is how you do it.

Why making sure people are always accompanied in everything they do is so important

Obviously, the harder we make the path, the fewer the people who can follow it, and the longer it will take us to get the income we want. The hardest path of all is the one which people walk alone. The easiest is the one you share with them and show them the way.

Mormons and Jehovah's Witnesses found out a long time ago that if people go out on their own, they will knock three to five doors and then give up. But two people going out together will knock 20, 30, 40 or more doors comfortably. And, what's more, they will keep going day after day. This is a dramatic increase in activity and a hefty reduction in the determination required to keep going.

I once was a door-to-door salesman, when such things were acceptable, and learnt for myself how important it is not to work on our own. The first company I joined did not allow salespeople out alone: you went out with someone more experienced than you, or you were training a new salesperson, or you were paired off with a colleague. We found it easy to do a lot of calls a day, and the company had quite a low drop out rate.

I then joined a new company which did not practise this system. Their drop out rate was very much higher; but what really surprised me, never having been out on my own before, was the effect on me of working by myself! I found the job very much harder. My work rate fell and I soon dropped out. I learnt that, when two people work together, each pushes the other's comfort zone out, but not just a little—a very long way.

> **When people work together, their work rate goes up astronomically.**

People working together reduces the talent and determination required to the minimum

If people work on their own, their talent and determination becomes important. So a group which allows this has to find highly self motivated people because it is the only way to generate group momentum. That is hard work: groups collapse because they cannot attract enough such people.

If people work together, the need for talent and determination reduce dramatically, and virtually anyone can succeed.

What if there is no upline to work with?

The amazing thing about people working together is that neither has to be good! If you cannot find an upline, find yourself another *new* distributor (often called a 'buddy') to work with. Anyone will do, they do not even have to be in your group.

Both your results and theirs will be far better, and you will both greatly reduce your chances of dropping out.

When your group starts growing, if an upline is not available to work with a new distributor (it is not always possible), find them a buddy to work with.

If you are new, you may worry about whether you are good enough to work this closely with your people. This is to misunderstand the purpose of working together. When I was selling door-to-door, some of the trainers who worked with me were, frankly, not much good. But we still sold much more than either of us would have done on our own, simply because our work rates were so much higher. No matter how inexperienced you are, you will do much more good for a new distributor by working with them than by not working with them.

Remember Zig Ziglar?: 'People do not care what you know, until they know that you care......about *them!*' The finest way to show your distributors that you care is to roll up your sleeves and get stuck in with them.

Two people working badly together will do at least ten times as well as each trying on their own, and will halve their chances of dropping out.

Where do you apply the rule of people being accompanied in everything they do?

Particularly, in four areas:

1. Get-Active phone calls
2. Two-to-ones
3. Registration meetings: when distributors sign up
4. Strategy meetings: when a new distributor's goals are discussed, their business strategy is planned, and they are put on the right lines

(5. If your product is suitable for parties, you should also accompany them while they are organising parties.)

> **Making sure people are always accompanied in everything they do is particularly important in relation to Get-Active phone calls**

Network marketing is all about 'knocking on doors' which, in our case, means Get-Active phone calls, and our experience is similar to that of the Mormons and Jehovah's Witnesses. If we let people make phone calls on their own, the great majority will make very few before dropping out.

If, however, we make sure that a new distributor always makes sponsoring calls with an upline or a buddy, 20 calls in an evening or during a couple of hours of the day is very achievable.

You can see that, contrary to what most people think, the most important reason why we work with an upline is not to learn from them. On the other side of the coin, the most important reason why we, as an upline, work with new distributors, is not to teach them:

> **The reason why we work together is to increase both their and our productivity**

The upline and the downline will both do significantly more *productive* work together than they will on their own. Not least, a good upline will keep the distributor they are working with off those non-IPA activities which we are all adept at finding to fill our time and pretend we are working!

This extra productivity also applies to the top distributors in your group. Even they will work a lot harder and a lot *better* when they are accompanying someone else (or if you accompany them).

Working together is also the fastest way to learn

Having said that the main reason for making sure that people are accompanied in everything they do is to increase productivity, a very important secondary purpose is that:

Working together is the fastest and the *only* effective way of learning

Teaching means hands on! If you wanted to learn how to drive a car, would you be happy if your instructor never actually got into a car with you, but thought it would be enough to teach in the classroom or over the phone? What would you think of a sports coach who never went out training with the people they were supposed to be coaching, but just used the phone, with maybe the occasional meeting in a hotel for a chat or a seminar?

Coaches have to *be* there with their people! Even the *top* teams and the *top* sportspeople will work a lot harder and a lot *better* if their coach is with them. If that is true for them then it is certainly true for everyone else!

On top of that, the more we work with people, the better we will become as teachers and the more we will learn about leadership. Therefore, even experienced distributors should never make Get-Active phone calls or do one-to-ones, registration meetings or strategy meetings (or, if relevant, organise parties) on their own, because not only are they missing valuable training opportunities, they are also missing opportunities to hone their skills of teaching and leadership.

Another excellent idea is for two *experienced* distributors to work together occasionally. By comparing notes, they will learn a lot from each other.

Accompanying people in everything they do gets us to a very important principle:

In network marketing, doing the job *is* teaching it, teaching the job *is* doing it

It can appear from the way we talk about teaching and leadership as if they are different functions to being a distributor. In almost every career or occupation you can think of, the leaders (usually called managers) and trainers are different people to those who do the job. In network marketing, we do not have this distinction. In other words,

There is no separation between being a distributor and being a teacher and leader.

Get classroom trainings into perspective

Although classroom trainings help, there is no substitute for on-the-job teaching

How many distributors actually do the job in the way they were shown in the classroom (or, for that matter, in books)? Almost none. So the value of classroom trainings is not in teaching people how to do the job. Their purpose should be seen only as providing the *framework* for what and how to do the job.

The great majority of uplines think that phone support is enough. It may suffice for giving advice, *but it is never the answer to increasing work rate, and it is never a substitute for proper teaching.*

Actually doing jobs *together* is the only way in which we can make sure things are done in the way we want them done, the only way in which we can make sure new people are taught in the way we want them taught, and is most certainly the only way to get the most work rate out of distributors. Classroom training and phone support have little value unless they are followed up in the field.

> Classroom training and phone support are back-ups for field training, and never ends in their own right.

What is the worst crime for leaders?

I said in *The Secrets Of Successful Sponsors* that you can never prejudge your contacts. The most important lesson we can learn from this chapter is that, actually, you can prejudge, because:

> Your best contacts are the ones who agree to let you accompany them in everything they do

As this is without question the biggest key to anyone's success, then it must be that the worst thing you can ever do as a leader is to make it acceptable for people to work unaccompanied. *Ban people from working on their own!*

Unfortunately in this there is a double problem: not only can it be difficult to get new distributors to agree to this, it can also be hard to get *uplines* to work this closely with their group. Don't worry about that, because the few people who will agree will have a dramatic affect on your group growth.

> Run your group with this philosophy: people working on their own is a killer

But one thing is for sure: if we ourselves do not consistently 'buddy' or work with other people, our people won't (the Theory of Duplication again: *People copy what you DO, not what you SAY*). Good leadership starts with *us* leading by example.

Chapter Twelve

How To Be A Great Teacher

The first rule of being a good teacher is to use your time in the most productive way for the benefit of your whole group.

This means: don't waste your time with people who do not want to learn! Who has earned the right to your time more, the person who wants to learn, or the person who does not? In fact,

> **Time spent with unteachable people is valuable time of which your teachable people are being deprived**

Anyway, which is the better use of your time?

Not everyone is teachable!

Two sorts of distributor will come into your group: teachable and unteachable. No matter how good a teacher you are, you can only teach people who want to be taught!

Even of those who are teachable, many will not carry what they learn into practice. So don't confuse a willingness to learn with a willingness to apply: someone who does not apply what they have learnt is going to be no more successful than someone who has not learnt in the first place, because:

> **Success comes from a distributor's *actions*, not from what they *learn*. The only learning which matters is that which is put into action**

Therefore:

Your purpose as a teacher is to get people to take action

Although a good teacher or leader might be able to convert some people from being unteachable to being teachable, or to convert others from inertia into action, it will not affect the overall position that by far the biggest reason for failure in your group will be people who are either unwilling to learn, or unwilling to do what is necessary to succeed.

So, whenever we refer to distributors, we are really only referring to those who will both learn and apply what they have learnt.

To this we must add **Consistency of Action.** This means that distributors should decide how much time they will devote to their business each week, *and then stick to it*. Consistency is so important because erratic work patterns never help anyone to get to where they want to go in business.

It is better to do less work consistently than to do more work in fits and starts

A distributor can of course vary the time they put in each week, provided that it is done in a planned way. If someone works only as and when they feel like it, there is little you can do to help them. In fact, distributors with the right success-attitude tend to put in more hours than they commit to.

You can therefore only *productively* apply your skills to people who:

      1. Will learn
      2. Will apply what they have learnt
      3. With consistency.

These are the only people you should work with. As I said before, they have earned the right to your time.

Value the slow learners

Contrary to what you might think, the talented fast learner often in the long run is not your best distributor. It is true that many such come into network marketing and take off like a rocket but, like a rocket, many of them fizzle out just as fast.

Go instead for the person who is keen to learn and will not give up. How talented or fast a learner they are does not come into it, because they are the ones who will make it long-term.

In fact, although it is painful for the slow learner (and sometimes, too, for the teacher!), being a slow learner often turns out to be a blessing in disguise because they tend to have more determination (they have to, to overcome their of lack of talent), and they often make good teachers. Because they found it hard to learn, they are more likely to be understanding of other slow learners.

Show complete confidence in a new distributor's success

New distributors often suffer from a crisis of confidence which, if not checked, will ruin their chances of success. This is not just the case with slow learners, or untalented people, or those who lack business experience. The most talented, experienced people can suffer as much, especially if their career path has been on a downward slide.

A distributor needs to see your complete confidence in them. If they feel that you have the slightest doubt, it will multiply out of all proportion in their mind. Even if you have no doubts about them, some distributors will create imaginary ones!

So be careful about how you phrase the points you want to make. Be careful not to guide them except in a positive, constructive way. Make sure that you listen carefully to what they have to say. Be sensitive to how they are feeling. Make it easy for them to open out their hearts and emotions to you.

The 'like—trust—respect' formula helps greatly in bolstering a distributor's confidence. But, most of all, look for compliments to pay them, and show your appreciation for their efforts.

> **People blossom when they feel you care about them, and when they feel valued and appreciated.**

Respect their efforts!

No matter how bad a job a new distributor is doing, no matter how unteachable they are and how much they think they know better, the purposes they want to achieve through your opportunity matter to them. So, no matter what you may think of their efforts, they are doing the best they know how. For that, they deserve your respect. And you stand more chance of getting them on track if you show that.

Don't forget how you felt when you started!

The beginning of a new distributor's career is a sensitive time, and we too often forget what it was like when we first started: the doubts we felt—the strangeness of a new career—our unfamiliarity with the product—how difficult we found the administration, the paperwork and a minefield of Dos and Don'ts—the problems that we had to overcome, perhaps the opposition of a loved one or a good friend—or the parts of the concept that we found difficult to grasp. All of these problems fade with experience and time, so that we can forget how much difficulty they caused us when we first started.

A new distributor needs to see that you know what it is like for them, and you won't if you have forgotten what it was like for yourself. With forgetfulness can come impatience—and an impatient teacher is a bad teacher.

Be a good example of your teaching

We have dealt with this before, but it bears repeating. If you try to get others to do what you are not doing yourself, you will build a whole group consisting of distributors who are telling everyone else what to do, but not doing it themselves. This is a problem. Any experienced distributor will tell you that most groups have a large number of people who suffer from this syndrome.

Make the teaching experience enjoyable!

Remember that most of your teaching is really doing the job: accompanying people on making Get-Active phone calls, doing 2-2-1s, running registration and strategy meetings and, if relevant, helping to organise parties. People will take their lead from you. If you make these activities heavy sessions, so will they. If you make them fun, so will they. This does not mean that you have to be creative or a laugh-a-minute comedian. It does mean that you should stay relaxed and light-hearted, and enjoy what you are doing.

Laugh at your mistakes! A new distributor may be worried about whether they can come up to expectations. They may also be worried about making a fool of themselves in front of you. Can you imagine the relief they feel when you admit to dropping a clanger and, even more, that you care little enough about it to find it funny? A trick of some experienced distributors is to deliberately make mistakes to help a new person feel at ease. Remember this:

> **No-one believes they can copy perfection, but everyone knows they can copy imperfection!**

If you are new and worried about whether you are good enough or experienced enough to teach a new distributor, this should make you, too, feel better. So if you make a mistake, so what? Who cares? Just get out there, work with your people and enjoy yourself, and it will all come right.

Chapter Thirteen

How To KISS. The Essence Of Great Teaching

Keep It Simple and Straightforward!

This is the **KISS Formula.** Remember what we said on page 25: if *the least experienced, least talented, least confident slowest learners in your group* cannot learn **and put into practice** what you teach, then your training needs reviewing. It is by keeping teaching simple that we make this a business for everyone. But there is a more important reason: to be successful, a new distributor is soon going to need to be able to teach others what you are teaching them now.

> A distributor cannot begin to be successful until they have learnt what, and how, to teach

The simpler you make the job, the more likely they will be to teach it in the way you want them to. So

> Even at the start, you are teaching every distributor to be a teacher.

1. Never teach more than the distributor can take in

In *The Secrets Of Successful Sponsors*, I said that when sponsoring you should unfold the business 'in bite sized chunks'. The same rule applies when you are teaching. Leaving aside how well you present information to them, two factors limit a person's ability to learn. One is the *speed* at which they can take in information. The second is the *amount* of information they can take in at any one time.

If you push a learning process too fast or try to give them more information than they can take, you will actually slow up their progress—it will take them longer to learn.

Pushing people too fast for themselves also undermines their belief in their ability to do the job. If we keep within a person's learning capability, the opposite happens. Their confidence increases as they find they can cope with what has to be learnt.

2. Don't assume a distributor knows

I well remember that in the first master classes I held, I worried that much of what I was saying was too obvious to justify my fee. It was only afterwards, when people came up to me to say how much they had learnt, that I realised that what was obvious to me was not necessarily obvious to other people. And many of these were very experienced distributors.

Most people do not like to admit their ignorance. If you assume knowledge which is not there, you can undermine their confidence in themselves. However, don't also assume an ignorance which is not there!

> *A town-dweller took up a new teaching post. As it was in a country school, he decided to plan his lessons around country animals. So he held up a cut-out of a sheep and asked the class, 'What is this?' There was silence. Amazed that country children did not know what a sheep looked like, he asked again. '***Surely*** *someone must know what this is?' A little boy tentatively put up his hand: 'Well,' he said, 'There's some Cotswold in it, and a little bit of Blackface. But I'm not sure about the rest.'*

3. Follow the Steps of Training

The easiest way to make something as simple as possible is to follow **the Steps of Training** when you are teaching:

⇒What to do

⇒How to do it

⇒Why it needs to be done

⇒Why it needs to be done in the way you are suggesting

⇒Check that it is understood

⇒Check that it is working.

You can do the steps above the line in any order, provided that you go through all four of them. Circumstances will dictate the best order to follow.

With regard to the last two steps, as teachers, we tend to assume that because we have explained something the other person must have understood it. Not always so! People often do not like to ask us to go more slowly or to go over something again in case we think they are stupid—or they may have genuinely thought they understood. So the onus is on us to make sure they have got the message correctly, by checking as we go along. It also brings to light if we are going too fast or trying to teach too much at one session.

There are many reasons why an idea we have taught may not work in practice. Sometimes, a distributor has misunderstood what we wanted them to do, sometimes an idea might work for us but it does not for them, sometimes we have got the circumstances wrong, and therefore our advice was wrong, sometimes the circumstances change, making our advice redundant. So follow up and check if a strategy is working. If it is not, the sooner we find out the sooner we can come up with an alternative solution.

4. Constant repetition, a necessary aid to KISS

The aim of good teaching is not only to impart information, it is to create the right habits of action. Habits only come from constantly repeated actions. If you need to break someone's bad habits, constant repetition is even more essential.

Even where retaining and remembering information is concerned, people rarely pick up everything a teacher wants them to from the first telling. Do you? Even the fastest learner will need to hear the same thing several times before they fully put it into practice the way you want them to. It is even more important where slow learners are concerned.

So keep repeating the message, or get distributors to constantly repeat the right way of doing things, until these become automatic. Once people know automatically, they can teach automatically. So constant repetition is a vital part of the teaching process. In fact, you cannot teach without it.

Patience

You can see that both the KISS Formula and constant repetition need patience. A good teacher is a patient teacher. Teaching slow learners also needs patience but, as we saw, it is patience well-placed.

Finally, never forget the golden rule of being a good teacher or leader: *Can the least experienced, least talented, least confident slowest learner follow me?* If the answer is yes, you've cracked it!

Chapter Fourteen

How To Be A Great Leader

As you can only teach people who want to be taught, so you can only lead people who want to be led. We said before that many distributors clasp their group closely to their breast as if the people in their group are their own personal property, and no-one else, especially uplines, can touch! We call them 'lone wolves'. They are not often successful and, more sadly, they rarely make good teachers, so the whole of that leg of your group is likely to be weak at best. Unfortunately, there is often not much you can do about it so, again, give your valuable time to those who deserve it: distributors who are grateful for your help.

Leadership is all about helping your people to achieve. All the great achievers in life, in whatever field of human endeavour, followed the same **Five Steps to Achievement:**

1. Inspiration
2. Focus
3. Passion
4. Planning
5. Drive.

You and all your distributors can follow the steps of these great men and women. These steps are available to all because achievement is nothing to do with intelligence, education, experience, wisdom or commonsense, character or personality, attractiveness, strength or stamina, background, sex, age or race. These attributes can, of course, help, but let's keep them in perspective:

> **There are very many people without any of these attributes who nevertheless achieve success; and there are very many people with all these attributes who never achieve success.**

Step one to achievement: Inspiration!

Achievement starts with the **inspiration** to achieve. Whether you are talking about great religious, political, business or military leaders, or great artists, writers or athletes, they all achieved because they were inspired to.

As distributors we, too, need to be inspired to reach the level we want to reach, and that is just as true whether we want a small, part-time income or aim to become the highest earner in our network. People only achieve to the level of their inspiration. If we are mightily inspired, we will achieve great things; if we are a little inspired, we will achieve little; if we are not inspired at all, we will never leave our beds.

What creates inspiration? A dream. But a dream that we are willing to fight for. I will show you now how to create that dream.

The dream of most people is to live life the way they want, whether this means academic life, status or materialism, a favourite pastime, a quest, the family, service to God, humankind or the natural world, or some combination of these. Whatever lifestyle you want, you will need the time to enjoy it and the money to fund it.

This is the **ATAC Lifeplan: A**bundant **T**ime, **A**bundant **C**ash: Abundant Time to be the person you want to be, do the things you want to do and have the things you want to have, and Abundant Cash to finance those aims. I call it the ATAC Lifeplan because the only way you are going to realize your Lifeplan is to ATTACK the things which get in the way of it.

Everyone will define their ATAC Lifeplan in a different way, so the first step is to define exactly what you mean by it.

What lifestyle would you like?

First, write down the answers to three questions:

- What sort of person would you like to be
- What would you like to do
- What would you like to have......

......if money was no object?

There is a difference between what you would like, and what you are prepared to work for. Many people would like to have a Rolls Royce or be a millionaire, but are they prepared to work hard for it? So cross off anything which does not inspire you to work, and this will leave you with an ATAC Lifeplan you are prepared to fight for. You now have the source of your inspiration.

Step two to achievement: Focus

How many dreamers do you know who never achieve what they want? Have *you* yet achieved what you want? So having a dream is not enough. Although it gives us the inspiration we need, it will not give us the success we want. That is because it is not the dream which decides the direction we take. It is our **focus** which decides our direction:

> **We get what we focus on in life, whether we want it or not**

The problem is that, although we often know what we want, we do not get it because we do not focus on it. To take a simple example, when you put food in the oven, is it not very important to you not to burn it? Yet how often has the doorbell gone, or you have decided to slip that little chore in and, before you know what has happened, your food has burnt? Didn't that make you furious? Well, if you were furious, it must have been very important to you not to burn it. But you still did. Why?

The human mind is so constructed that it has to focus on something and, if we do not focus on what we want (unburnt food), our focus will go elsewhere and we will get what we do not want (burnt food). But notice something else:

If we do not focus on what we want, our focus is always high-jacked by something *less* important

The doorbell going or that little chore you did were not at that moment as important as not burning the food, yet that is what you got. If we want success, we must learn to keep focused on what we want.

So how do we avoid our focus being high-jacked by less important things? We create our **FOOD Card.** What does that mean? **FO**cus **O**f **D**esire, which we shorten to FOOD, because your Focuses of Desire *are* your food of life, the food of your success, the reason why you try to achieve anything.

Get a 4" x 6" index card, and from your ATAC Lifeplan choose and write down between one and four objects which symbolise the lifestyle you want. We call these your **Focuses of Desire,** because you are now going to focus on these as the good things in life you want from your network marketing business. Your Focuses of Desire do not have to be material objects, they can be support of a favourite cause or whatever you want. But they must be something you badly want and can see with crystal clarity in your mind's eye.

Every morning, *rewrite* your FOOD Card. The card is not big (which is why I suggest it), so this will not take long, but it will help to imprint your Focuses of Desire deep into your being.

During the day, pull out your FOOD Card as often as you can, especially when you feel tired, demotivated or filled with doubt. But don't just read it, because that will achieve nothing. Achievement comes from *visualising* and *feeling* all the nice emotions you will have from ownership of the objects or purposes you have chosen, and of the ATAC Lifeplan they conjure up for you. In other words,

Read with feeling. Visualise ownership

It will add clarity and energy to your visualisations if you use a photo or some other visual reminder of each of your Focuses of Desire.

If any of the Focuses of Desire ceases to motivate you, it is not as important to you as you thought. Replace it with another which does excite you.

By knowing precisely what our ATAC Lifeplan is and continuously focusing on it, we create the means to get there. By knowing precisely what we want from life and continuously focusing on it, we create the means to get it.

Step three to achievement: Passion

Passion is another source of inspiration. The more passionately we feel about someone, the more we will do for them. Feel passionately enough about something, and we want to spend all our time doing it. And the more passion we feel, the better we do our job.

So what can you feel passionately about? Obviously, first of all your ATAC Lifeplan and the Focuses of Desire on your FOOD Card because, if you are not passionate about them, you have the wrong ones. But beyond that you should feel passionately about **your product** and how it can enhance people's lives; **your opportunity** and the concept of **network marketing,** which together can help people to achieve what they want. Finally, you should feel passionate about **the success of your distributors,** the people who come into your group trusting you to show them the way.

The more you are passionate about what you do, the quicker you will realize your ATAC Lifeplan. The way to do this is to keep focused on *why* you love this great business of ours. Write down all the good things about your opportunity, and keep focused not on the things you do not like (which is what most of us do!) but on what you do like about it. Now read this often.

Some people need the income from their network marketing business to fund their present lifestyle. If that applies to you, write down all the things you love about your life right now, and which your business will allow you to maintain. Now read this often. And remember to keep focused on your FOOD Card, because your network marketing business is the way you have chosen to achieve all those aims.

Step four to achievement: Planning

If you fail to plan, you are planning to fail

Many people fail because they do not *plan* how they are going to achieve success. The steps you need to take are:
1. Work out how much you will need to earn from your network marketing business to realize your ATAC Lifeplan, and by when you want to earn that figure
2. Next, break that target down to what you have to earn each month from now until your target is reached
3. Finally, at the beginning of each month, plan what you are going to do *each day* to hit the target for that month.

Step five to achievement: Drive

Drive is essential to achievement. It means going for what we focus on with determination and a sense of urgency. It is by focusing on what inspires us that we create the enthusiasm and the energy we need to get to where we want to go. The more we focus on bringing our dreams to life, the more Drive, enthusiasm and energy we will create to turn those dreams into reality. The less we focus on them, the less we will do to achieve them. So,

---
Inspiration + Focus *creates* Drive

The purpose of the Five Steps to Achievement is to create Focus and Drive. In network marketing, just as in any part of life, how far you go will be determined by your Focus and Drive: focusing on what inspires you, and driving yourself to achieve it.

The more Focus and Drive you have, the further and faster you will go
---

It is amazing how far people with Focus and Drive can go, even with very little knowledge! Many top distributors got there in just this way. However, the opposite is not true: I know of *no* distributor whose sheer depth of knowledge made up for a lack of Focus and Drive.

Focus and Drive can compensate for lack of knowledge; but knowledge cannot compensate for a lack of Focus and Drive
---

Yes, you should acquire as much knowledge of your subject as you can. Yes, you should do the right things in the right way. *But without Focus and Drive, they will not get you far.*

Teach your people how to inspire themselves

If all your people are constantly focusing on what success in your opportunity will give them, how much will you have to motivate them to succeed?

If the only thing you ever do in network marketing is to *continuously* impress on your people the power of Inspiration, Focus and Drive, you will be amazed at what you can achieve.

How to turn dreams into reality

The Five Steps to Achievement can be summed up as:

Decide exactly what you are going for. Decide exactly how to go for it.

THEN JUST GO FOR IT!

'What Do I Do Next?'

With the benefit of the previous chapter, we need to change your expectation of the people you will be prepared to work with. We call this **The On-Track Formula.** The distributors to whom you should give most of your effort are those who:

1. Will learn from you
2. Will apply what they have learnt *with Focus and Drive*
3. And with consistency......

......because these are going to be your best people, your top teachers and leaders.

The biggest lessons to take away from this book are:

1. Making sure people that are accompanied in everything they do is essential (*Ban people from working on their own*)
2. That you should be the best example you can be of what you are teaching and of what leadership is all about
3. The more you care for, support and respect the distributors in your group, the more successful you will be.

You have now worked through the first four books in *The Secrets Series* on how to create and run a successful network marketing business: *Just What Is...... Network Marketing?*, *The Distributor's Action Plan*, *The Secrets Of Successful Sponsors* and *The Secrets Of Successful Teachers & Leaders*.

Structuring your group in the right way, and understanding the mathematics of network marketing which goes with it, can literally make the difference between your success and failure. It will definitely make a major difference to how long it takes you to get to the income you want. It is a vital skill to learn, and it is a vital skill to teach your people. So the next stage is to learn how best to structure your group, and we will cover that in the next and last title in *The Secrets Series*, *The Secrets Of Successful Group Structuring*.

As I said in the Introduction, personal development is also an essential skill. If you are not yet reading a book on personal development (perhaps either of my two: *Network Marketeers ... Supercharge Yourself!* or *How To Achieve Everything You've Ever Wanted*), now is the time to do so.

Good teaching and leadership is all about teaching your people to do what you have just done. So they should be following you through *The Secrets Series*. Apart from anything else, it makes your life much easier if you give the distributors in your group the same grounding of knowledge as you have had. Having a common culture of training makes everyone's success more certain, including yours.

I hope that our journey together through this book has made you confident that not only can you be a great teacher and leader, but that you can teach the least experienced, least talented, least confident slowest learners how they, too, can be great teachers and leaders.

And keep making people feel the better for you passing by!

By David Barber on network marketing

The *Secrets* Series
Just What Is... Network Marketing?
The Distributor's Action Plan
The Secrets Of Successful Sponsors
The Secrets Of Successful Teachers & Leaders
The Secrets Of Successful Group Structuring

The STARSS Leadership Programme
Get Off To A Winning Start In Network Marketing
Breakthrough Sponsoring & Retailing
How To Lead A Winning Group
Network Marketeers...... Target Success!
Network Marketeers...... Supercharge Yourself!

Other titles
Network Marketing: A Different Way Of Doing Business
How To Give The Best Parties On The Block!
The Daily Express Guide To Network Marketing
(published By Kogan Page)

Group discounts
Are you a group leader? If so, we can supply you with books to sell to your people at exceptional discounts. For full details, contact the publishers:

Cedar Publishing Limited
12 Pitch View
46 Kingsholm Road
Gloucester
GL1 3AU
01452 523727.